The Daughters of Discordia

The Daughters of Discordia

poems by

Suzanne Owens

Foreword by Denise Duhamel

BOA Editions, Ltd. ❧ Rochester, NY ❧ 2000

LC #: 00–131755
ISBN: 1–880238–89–6 A paperback original

First Edition
00 01 02 03   7 6 5 4 3 2 1

Publications by BOA Editions, Ltd.—
a not-for-profit corporation under section 501 (c) (3)
of the United States Internal Revenue Code—
are made possible with the assistance of grants from
the Literature Program of the New York State Council on the Arts,
the Literature Program of the National Endowment for the Arts,
the Sonia Raiziss Giop Charitable Foundation,
the Eric Mathieu King Fund of The Academy of American Poets,
The Halcyon Hill Foundation, as well as from
the Mary S. Mulligan Charitable Trust, the County of Monroe, NY,
Towers Perrin, and from many individual supporters.

*   *   *

See Colophon Page
for Acknowledgement of Special Individual Supporters.

Cover Design: Rishma Goa
Cover Art: "Persephone's Window," Xerographic Transfer
on Paper and Canvas, 1995, by Suzan Woodruff, Courtesy of Richard Foerster.
Typesetting: Richard Foerster, York Beach, Maine
Manufacturing: McNaughton & Gunn, Lithographers
BOA Logo: Mirko

BOA Editions, Ltd.
Steven Huff, Publisher
Richard Garth, Chair, Board of Directors
A. Poulin, Jr., President & Founder (1976–1996)
260 East Avenue
Rochester, NY 14604

www.boaeditions.org

CONTENTS

ॐ

FOREWORD

Terrorists. Sex spies. Sea witches. Heretics. Bank robbers. Slaves. Serial killers. Suffragettes. These are just some of the women we hear from in *The Daughters of Discordia*, Suzanne Owens's series of gritty persona poems that challenge what exactly "yin" is and explore the dark and violent interiors of the feminine psyche. Hers is a revisionist poetry—reclaiming, inventing, and rediscovering the voices of "the malodorous / women of crime: servant, orphan, spinster / herded, prodded, chained together." Owens frees these women to sing—some from the grave—and turns point of view on its head. The poems in this book, frightening and tender, serve as footnotes for history books and marginalia for contemporary tabloids.

What makes these poems "poems," rather than interesting pieces of regained news, is Owens's precise ear and gift for detail. In "The Disappearing Woman" she writes, "My conversion vanished when you took / my feather dress and sent it to the Vatican." In "The Banishment" we read, "Honey does not make a king. Beware the bee-eater." Her acute imagery and the authority with which she delivers a line are remarkable.

Owens's shifts from poem to poem, from character to character, is exciting and authentic. Here she gives voice to 1930s scrappy Ma Barker:

> . . . When my Freddy and his lover
> Karpis—we called him Creepy after his facial alteration—
> when they weren't knocking over banks they were
>
> scouting out young gals to bring home
> for me to knock around. Devoted to their Ma, they were.
> When I finished having sex I'd say, Get rid of her, boys.
>
> They'd just up and kill her .

To facilitate the story of Elizabeth Parsons Ware Packard ("The Watch Book"), incarcerated in a mental hospital in 1863, Owens uses an entirely different stylistic approach: "My clothes were taken, / the key, the door locked. No key / could fit my mouth."

In telling these stories, Owens seems less interested in the victim/perpetrator dichotomy than with a spectrum of behavior that mixes the two. This spectrum is most apparent in Owens's preoccupation with mothers who kill their own children. She includes the voices of farmgirls and slaves, and, perhaps most chillingly, modern-day women. In "Nine Stones," Owens imagines the murders (from 1972 to1985) of all nine of Marybeth Tinning's children. The poet does not shy away from Tinning's madness:

> . . . Suspicion blisters
>
> In gobs: Desitin cream daubed on
> Like glue, a pillow laid over a rash,
> A mouth festering beneath. *Babies cry*
> *TOO MUCH.* . . .

Owens gives us as a last line to section four of "Nine Stones"—the elegy for Timothy Tinning—"*Every funeral is a party.*"

Owens's book is full of such small painful ironies. In "The Arsenic Eater," when Hannah Kinney is acquitted for killing her two husbands, the "courtroom crowd [rises] up / and [cheers] to the 'law's chivalry,' " and in "The Snow-White Dove: Hapless, Helpless, and Forlorn," Ann Simpson, who poisoned her husband in 1850, flies "to the jury's bosom. / They weren't so dastardly to hang a woman." Contrast those sentiments with "Suffrage, 1917: Imprisoned for Obstructing Traffic," in which the suffragette speaker is fearless of "the spoonfuls of worms I scoop / from the surface of my soup every day," while her nurses are convinced she suffers from "persecution mania." The laws of nature, governments, and religions are random in *The Daughters of Discordia*.

Owens's treatment of Cattle Kate, a cattle rustler who was lynched in 1889 ("Homestead Claim No. 2003"), dwells not on her grisly death but instead on Cattle Katie's frontier entrepreneurial skills: "they'd drive a stolen heifer over / to my ranch and trade it for a little ass." Owens takes an unusual approach to sex and violence—unusual because in the following three poems the women are *committing* the violence. In "The KGB Sex School for Spies: Men Called 'Ravens,' Women 'Swallows,' " Owens writes:

> Little swallows, well trained in the arts
> Of deviation: vodka, caviar, gifts;
> We undressed, learned to stroll
>
> In front of the class, practiced contrived
> Passion, darting, swooping, infrared
> Before the two-way mirrors.

Belle Gunness, serial killer born in 1860, also lures men with promise of her sexuality. In "My Heart Beats in Wild Rapture for You: Come Prepared to Stay Forever," Owens has Gunness explain herself like this:

> No vile despoilers
> answered my honey-kissed ad.
> They dug out their lives' savings
>
> from the local banks as boggle-eyed
> as the deputies who unearthed
> the bones and eleven men's watches
> in my hog pen.

And in "Kim's Story" North Korean terrorist Kim Hyon Hui, who places a bomb on a South Korean airliner, killing 116 people, is seen as attractive because of it:

> each day they forward my mail:
> marriage proposals, death threats,
> invitations to tea. Men want me.
> I am a Virgin Terrorist.

Women's "power" and prowess are everywhere among *The Daughters of Discordia* who are fighters and engage in all kinds of magic. In "The Sea Witch of Billingsgate: To Her Betrayer," a farmgirl, supposedly given powers by the devil, casts a spell on the one who has sexually abused her then abandoned her, wishing that she "will lock your pirate's legs / in a fish-tail." She tells him, "I will cut up tempests / around your ship, hurricanes."

In "My Father Sold Me to Pay His Debts," Owens, using the voice of slave who has been raped by her owner, writes: "With lightning in my apron, / I stole from my master's home / at midnight." And in "The Miserable Sinner," a slave—who had been raped by a white man and then has killed their baby—on her way to her death says, "I may be slave but walk as queen behind my own / procession."

Discordia, "goddess of error," reigns over all that happens in this book. I am grateful to Suzanne Owens for unearthing these stories and transforming them into such tragic and regal poems.

—*Denise Duhamel*

for Evangelene and Cullen

ONE: THE INSTIGATOR

THE BANISHMENT

Zeus banished Discordia, one of his daughters, because she caused vengeance, greed, and war among the gods. He sent her to earth to hurl man into disaster.

Whom else have you expelled like a Titan forever
Wild and powerless to return? Fate will devour you
As your father swallowed his children.

Wasn't I born Discordia, goddess of error?
Have I caused more havoc than my sisters: Sorrow,
Slaughter, Famine, Murderous Quarrel?

Wasn't the daughter of night, mother of lawlessness,
My mother, too? I never claimed the golden apple.
You were nourished on nectar from rare beehives.

Honey does not make a king. Beware the bee-eater.
Balance your light. Remember Hades, invisible
By his magic helmet. You breathe his air, as I do,

Curdling into the human: the tin-lidded
Flesh-stench, strife-broken clay, the mock trial.
Like the valley, I am jealous

Of the mountain. My view thickens. I watch
The clear light of Olympus narrow.
Nutshell-huddled sheds take shape. I taste

Vineyards, wool, bondage. Sweat mists
The rivers, Sadness and Lamentation.
Into what new fires can I pitch the mortal,

What unaccountable nights? Haven't you yourself
Unblessed the deathlings with afterworlds they will
Unleash inside themselves, useless to forestall?

Poor momentaries—creatured to perish. Even I,
The one who sets the moon afire, who consumes coral,
Its poison exuding from my skin, plead

Isn't it enough, to dole out entire shares
Of lightning bolts from clay pots that stand
Left and right like sentinels by your palace door?

৶

TWO: THE ACT

DIFFICULT

*Neighbors and the state authorities were convinced
that Dorothy Talbye was possessed by Satan. She was
hanged in Boston, 1638.*

What I could not do in life,
I do in death: snatch the cloth
off my face, tuck it
under the noose to ease the vise.

I lose me slowly as the old
lose words, names of my only
possessions: Indian corn,
canoe, tub, ax, spinning wheel.

Clickity-clack. My name is
printed. My name is ink.
They knew me as "The Godly One."
But the court said

I laid hands on my husband,
endangered his life,
and he paid twenty bushels
of good leaf tobacco for me, too.

Publicly whipped. I lost
the name of a friend, objects
I covet: kid boots, a bonnet.
I would not go back to church.

God spoke to me through
the chants of my spinning.
I prayed for my tiny girl,
the one I named Difficult

because I knew how her life
would be. It was God who said,
Don't leave Difficult here
in this misery,

so I broke her neck. Bound,
chained to a post, I forgot
the names of those I loved,
finally their faces. I walked

away. I would not listen.
It took three big ones
to hold me, to make me stand
to hear it.

Excommunication.
They wrenched my shoulders,
yanked my arms.
I would not stand up.

I would not confess.
Repent. Repent. I swing
a few times back and forth
still trying to catch

the ladder. In the name
of all I possess: canoe, tub, ax,
spinning wheel,
I will not. Clickity. Clack.

ॐ

SHEEP AND FODDER

In the late 1600s women convicts were often trans-
ported from England to the Massachusetts colonies;
during the two-month crossing, roughly one-third of
the prisoners would die.

Here's a prayer from a spry old tit:
she wants to thank You for Your blessings.
This year old man winter lived like me:
beyond his time. But I'm not ready
to go yet. Getting married tomorrow,
my sixth husband and him a slice my age.
You know, it's not the number of years
that matter here, it's the size of your estate.

I've seen them all pass on, those
reeking women of Newgate: Jane,
fair, fat, and lusty, smoking tobacco, her teeth,
black all along the jawbone; Ann,
pitted with smallpox; Betty, that masculine
wench, her leg in a horse-lock and chain.
No one walked by our foul prison unless
they had to. The name of our boat: *Charity,*

a portent for me, but not for old Mary Lou,
hanged, thrown into the sea
to appease the storm. Witches, dry peas,
salt pork, and gin. Did we rile the men?
Down there in the fetid hold, sheep and fodder
more welcome than us, the malodorous
women of crime: servant, orphan, spinster
herded, prodded, chained together.

Better than slow starvation to be taken
across the water as servants, then courted.
We didn't need to buy our husbands.
We were bought. But God, have mercy
on those without hope, good-wishes,
or prayers who murdered themselves.
Some of us lived to be necessary;
we were better than none.

ಎ

THE MISERABLE SINNER

*Alice Clifton, a sixteen-year-old black slave was raped
by a white man called Shaffer. She told the doctor
that Shaffer had ordered her to kill the baby.*

I am a child of chance with a window brush
as talisman, tossing my head, my hair tangly
in the shadow of smoke signals, less meaningful
than the words rising above that mountain.

I have lost myself much. A cloak makes its entrance.
It is on Sunday, the day for the reverend,
more concerned with his own voice rumbling
than with God's or mine. As silent as ice melt,

I am debauched in the alley by fat Shaffer,
the cockalorum. He tells me where to put my mouth.
Like fruit, stars fall into the river. They fill the sockets,
the eyes of babies, fish-plucked flowers.

Those flowers spill their pollen that lands, by chance,
on the knife he orders me to hold above my head.
Here's a plate, frayed at the edges, cracked
to the center holding a scratch of blood and whiskers

able to do their mending work. The butter churns.
I know the keepers at home sit with their thighs spread.
Virginity does not keep until it turns rancid, nor women
reared for death who melt away like the moon

a mile out of town, their coffins raised before them.
I may be slave but walk as queen behind my own
procession. Because this rope adapts with ease looped
around my neck, don't think I have not drawn

the Circle around myself. Tip cut from a wolf's penis,
locusts from around his eyes. Even though my casket,
nailed rough, hewn with indifference, may not be
bird-carved with angel drawings,

I draw Power. I walk barefoot.

MY FATHER SOLD ME TO PAY HIS DEBTS

During their seven-year bondage, indentured servants
were forbidden to marry. If they became pregnant, their
servitude could be lengthened by at least two years.
Some masters would rape them in order to extend it.

I lacked beauty, the graces,
a chaste mien. No husband
wanted me. I was the albatross,
the superfluous daughter

who sailed with the maimed,
the well bred and modest, whore
and murderess alike to a place
where heaven was a blanket

and the ground to lie upon,
where hope was a river packet:
mail and cargo on the Mississippi
or a pair of scissors to cut

our throats, to stab our bellies with.
We were raped by our masters,
worked, whipped, dragged
through the streets behind carts,

through the river in the boat's wake,
held under water until
we were dead. Fear
wrote the laws. Their pits and snares

cumbered us: sermons, records. . . .
We dug the pits in our gardens,
and barns, snared forbidden
pregnancies under our skirts.

With lightning in my apron,
I stole from my master's home
at midnight, labored alone
in the winter field. Others

retired with headaches
to second-floor bedrooms
while the families ate, smothered
their babies with pillows,

dropped them down wells,
into rivers. We have seen
the fire hanging above the lake,
embraced the Druid women

as we burned at the stake. I stood
with the rope round my neck.
From the fire under me, the hand
of my dead master flared up,

grabbed the rope over my head.
Lit it.
I fell alive into the flames.
Still struggling.

≈♥

THE SEA WITCH OF BILLINGSGATE:
TO HER BETRAYER

*Seduced and abandoned by the pirate Black Sam
Ballamy and imprisoned for killing their baby, Goody
Hallett of Cape Code was mysteriously freed. The
legend has it that she was responsible for sinking
Ballamy's ship in 1717.*

I can see you, Black Ballamy, through
the glass eye of my gray goat. Sail
the *Whidah* with your crew
farther than the sun dares; the maid

you ruined under the Wild Plum
will lock your pirate's legs
in a fish-tail. You will sing mer-songs
to the lobsters. When the fog makes

arc-shapes with the shoals: hips,
shoulders, the form a girl takes
lying in a barn, I will cut up tempests
around your ship, hurricanes. You will gaze

spellmoored at the granite as I did
at the stranger wearing French bombace
who freed me. I touched his gold quill
to my tongue, drew my mark

with a slantendicular X. The scarlet tip
glittered. No black art of yours will flick
the reefs away like stray bits of rye-straw
as he flicked away my prison bars, tapped

the silver darbies on my wrists with his cane—
I live in Leviathan. A ship's light flies
from his tail. Contracharms will not rid
the hymn-bellowers of me. Let all men stick

pins in calves' hearts, drop the hearts down
every chimney in town. I am a deep-dyed
sinner, a white girl, a red girl. I have more lives
than my familiar. Some nights, I lure

a skipper or a young hand to the lorn hut
on the poverty-grass meadow. On occasion,
some return before cockcrow withered and creak-
jointed. Watch for the glimpse of my heels.

ॐ

GOD IS A COWBOY WHO RIDES A LAME HORSE

Adoniram Burroughs, bookeeper, left Iowa for Wash-
ington, D.C., after sexually abusing Mary Harris for
five years. Still, he promised to marry her on her eigh-
teenth birthday. Instead, he wed a Washington so-
cialite. When her breach-of-promise suit failed, Har-
ris shot Borroughs in Washington. At the trial in 1865
she was judged insane, and at twenty sentenced to an
asylum in Baltimore to recuperate.

Burroughs fondled me in the store's back room
where I worked with the fancy goods
when I was three cents a day
and nine years old.

Here, in this paper, I read the news
of his wedding. My twitches
feed the carpet berry juices. They say it is
my monthly blood that holds me

on the winter floor nights, my blood
that tears clothes, rips books.
The doctor sees it in my wild eye, my womb
gone mad. I hear its curses in the racketing

of each railway tie all the way to Washington
racing God who loathes me.
My nervous symptoms clutch his love letters
five years, stamped with

"mourning for our stolen kisses." I lift
my green veils. Shots. Their destination through
the corridors as confident as Sherman's army
marching to the sea. My four-barrel pistol speaks twice;

Burroughs falls in the hall of the Treasury building—
his eyes, their blue so pale, I can see right through
to his vows to make me "a very seemly wife."
Mold the tankard, fill it, drink the glistening.

***

My borrowed money; it's twelve-hour days
that wear bare feet and go hungry; he sinks
whiskeylogged into Miss Boggs, their wedding,
soft Washington society.

Our two bastard babies in the west: the first,
his neck I twisted, a sprig buried in a stall
warming beneath the cow's belly; the other,
as light as paper money, a rolled wad

in Burroughs's pocket. The one whose skull
I leaned my elbow on, shoved
into a pit, lies there still pastured
under the sage. A Confederacy surrenders.

Oh, my heart's lust, my bruised apron,
my weighted pincushion. How they fly.
A bleak cloak and stillborn promises
swathe me in "no guilt." Veils

never again to be lifted over my head.
Against my breast, my hands crush the flowers
poor Mrs. Lincoln sent. In the crowd of jurors
who acquitted me, little stone hands

wave my carriage on to the depot. No hands
can redress the rents made in the barn's sweat,
the fermented pasture. Baltimore did not
recuperate my straggling hair, my breached life.

HOMESTEAD CLAIM NO. 2003

The lynching of Ella Watson, known as Cattle Kate,
in 1889 triggered the Johnson County war between
the powerful Wyoming Stock Growers Association
and the small independent ranchers.

I was just another cattle rustler, hell
with a six-gun, queen of the branding iron
and lariat. They called me the devil
in the saddle, a terror astride a bronc,

the best little whore in Johnson County.
From the outlaw's hideout, Hole-in-the-Wall,
they'd drive a stolen heifer over
to my ranch and trade it for a little ass. Vigilantes

danced in the hall, the king of the rustlers
played his fiddle. My herd increased.
I applaud the ones who apply
their own brand. Life is nothing

but a pilfered animal. I took whatever
came my way: a pair of fancy horses,
a silver-studded saddle. We're here no longer
than the time it takes to hear a six-gun barking,

the groan of a hollow barn, the flap
of bleached slats swinging in the storm. So,
noose my neck to the cottonwood branch.
Watch my knickers kick the air.

A few maverick cattle wind up
in everyone's corral. Some kind of lariat
is finally tossed. We're all driven
to the railhead for shipment.

❧

THE KGB SEX SCHOOL FOR SPIES: MEN CALLED "RAVENS," WOMEN "SWALLOWS"

In the Soviet school for sex spies young, patriotic members of the party or criminals, prostitutes, and homosexuals were "chosen" or forced into the job by threat of imprisonment. One former swallow became a double agent for the CIA. But in 1971 her duplicity was discovered by the KGB bosses.

It was either The House of Love,
Prison, or something far more deadly
Than humiliation. Obedient

Little swallows, well trained in the arts
Of deviation: vodka, caviar, gifts;
We undressed, learned to stroll

In front of the class, practiced contrived
Passion, darting, swooping infrared
Before the two-way mirrors.

There were precarious defectors,
Suicides, and double agents,
parts of me found in suitcases:
Amputated legs in one, torso in another. . . .

***

Like Delilah, I was sent to you.
Armed with custom-made handbag,
Its false compartment filled

With compromise, knowledge of your
Taste for women and your secret
Perversions. More than a beauty

With brains, a large apartment,
I was a code name with fringe benefits
Long before I walked into that bar.

Our chance meeting. It was all staged.
Even my husband's onetime interruption
In the well-bugged love nest,
Pretending outrage.

***

How well we pleased each other: my prey,
My game, my weanling ruin.
We made treason

In every court, a bright speed-film
Flying between the east, the west
Of that erotic bed. You craved me

More than reputation, power, fable. . . .
My feathers preened. Fine oils.
The only wires

I really needed. No use
The closed curtain, a chair rammed
Under the handle of the bedroom door,
The dark.

***

Those seconds of your satisfied flesh
That triggered the transmitter
I was forced to ingest.

Recordings: your voice, drawings,
Confidential files flashed. I turned your
Classified face toward the camera concealed

In the wall: nests of tapes. Those perfect
Exposures in illicit. Then a shrug of blackmail,
My double-dealing wings. Our agreement

In a spasm convulsing
With silver pieces. . . . Like Rahab, I lied.
I was sent from the city with my possessions,
And all was slaughter.

❧

NINE STONES

At first some doctors, caseworkers, friends and neighbors thought that Marybeth Tinning's children died from genetic causes, others presumed sudden infant death syndrome. Suspicions grew, but nothing could be proved at the time. On Friday, July 17, 1987, she was diagnosed with Munchausen syndrome by proxy and sentenced to twenty years for the murder of her last child, Tami Lynne.

1. Jennifer Tinning (December 26, 1971 to January 3, 1972)

You were the first to feel the soft pillow
Of no-breath, to see my eye-glaze,

Over-a-shoulder look at the wall; you never
Played with sparrows in treehouses, never

Touched the bagatelle on the evergreen.
Just a portrait of a little lamb on metal.

My curve delivered to the bells near
Your heart. One pure motion struck

Your arch of leaves, your table of flurry,
Bypassed cities running through the rivers

Tangled in your eyes. You live in my
Remembering: warped, decried, wanting

Your hair brown. You live with the comets,
Gone from the planet, synapses, ligaments freed.

2. Joseph Tinning (January 10, 1970 to January 20, 1972)

You were a cap of bells, a fold
At the end of my sleeve wearing the wilt

Of white snow. With a tear in my skirt of skin
I threw down the yarrow. What did you think

I would be: a diamond, a decade, a cosmic
wind field? Once I dislodged the percussion cap,

You were gone like winter into the ground
As if you had never happened.

Even before the wake, I dumped your toys,
Your clothes, your straggle into a pillowcase

Still damp with breath from an airway
Too small to struggle. I was the warden:

Same gray coat, same fox fur locking up.
You were Saturday night after calamity.

3. Barbara Tinning (May 31, 1967 to March 2, 1972)

I aided nurses, drove the school bus. Now
I collect big tips at the Flavorland restaurant.

When I hang my head, whisper like a child
Who would guess I got away with it.

One time, I left you careless
On the counter stool. You toppled off. I stood,

A propped menu, a child's flat drawing
Holding merely a premonition of perspective

While the doting waiters hoped
You would live beyond five.

The barmaid's mission,
To give me a doll like you: strawberry blond,

Innocent smile, porcelain face, pink dress—
A flea-market tip of her sneaking suspicion.

4. Timothy Tinning (November 21, 1973 to December 10, 1973)

Suspicion is not a mysterious disease.
It turns up like heat, an odd sock,

Music from a stuffed moonman, coins
In a shoe. Suspicion blisters

In gobs: Desitin cream daubed on
Like glue, a pillow laid over a rash,

A mouth festering beneath. *Babies cry
TOO MUCH.* I block my ears with

Afternoon bars, someone's pilfered
Purse, motel rooms *du jour,*

The Duanesburg truck stop. Your father
Stands, an extraneity

Fully dressed by your bassinet shaking
His head. *Every funeral is a party.*

5. Nathan Tinning (March 30, 1975 to September 2, 1975)

Two minutes of force while your father sleeps.
Two minutes of thrashing arms, legs.

The mobile's music twists the air. I can't resuscitate
The right street number. The ambulance gets

Lost. I lose myself in the living room,
Pace the windows wringing my crib deaths

While the milk on the counter rests in day-to-night
Thicken. I confess to your skin, a little pale.

Only God knows what happened,
The doctor says, slumping into the chair. Only

Stones know the color of my lowered eyes
While you sleep to the calls of the usual, nocturnes plucked

On a question piping agape from the parlor walls.
Even my hair casts its shadow.

6. Mary Francis Tinning (October 29, 1978 to February 22, 1979)

The apnea monitor, left in the armchair,
Did not sound its alarm at the pause

Of her heartbeat. In a heartbeat,
She was under the ground. I punched out

My little-girl whisper-calls: my list
Of telephone numbers, *just thought friends*

Should know. I wanted you to be the first
To hear it. I wanted her name inscribed,

But she was an *Et al.*, and *Daughter* was all
She got. He scratched the ice off

Each plaque, like he scratched off
Partial payments, three funerals in a row.

The ladies came carrying great importance
On platters of baked cookies, in ham casseroles.

7. Jonathan Tinning (November 19, 1979 to March 24, 1980)

You were the proof of someone's
Backseat-of-a-car virility, an auto-garage

Memory of erotica conceived with tires,
Wrenches, pumps. I was the child in the last row,

My face turning into the shape of my shoes,
The bus monitor who yelled at smaller children,

Screamed at those too old to boss, daughter
Of the punch press operator, his voice forever

Raised, his harshness outlined behind the screen.
I am the woman in the last cell. Caseworkers

Fear me, inmates retreat to yell their gospels—
I am your mother, No. 80, who draws a finger

Over her mouth. *We need duct tape here.*
That's what we need. DUCT TAPE.

8. Michael Tinning Adopted (August 3, 1978 to March 2, 1981)

Not even your mixed skin could keep you
Downwind of me. No death gene in this
Tiny, perfect body lying still
On the metal table. Your step-father went back
To bed after the hospital declared you dead;
Your passing as common as a linen-weave drape.
Another funeral notice, another deluge
On the Hot Line: Was the house searched,
Air tested, heat ducts clean?
No trauma, no fall, no bruise. No case for court.
Another infant Jesus freezes on his
Sculpted cribstone. A black man,
A white woman slip in before the mourners arrive,
Gaze at your open casket, overstuffed with toys.

9. Tami Lynne Tinning (August 22, 1985 to December 20, 1985)

No root to a spring frost. No proof
To a smother. I knew how to do it.

The doctor couldn't tie my hands.
Asked if he could tie my tubes. *Done*

I told him from my binary mouth
Feeling the ninth importance, reliving

The first consciousness out of earshot
As my underground stem, set with eyes,

Tubered death again. Only me there
At the end, with the "baby-spot-of-mystery"

On the crib sheet. Another all-night
Hospital wait-in-a-cot. The last casket

Opens crammed with toys. A fugitive daughter
From Elysium has left her dower of resin.

≈

THREE: THE CELL

THE DISAPPEARING WOMAN

For 4,000 years the Chumash Indian tribe consisting
of sixty-eight villages lived on San Nicolas Island off
the coast of California. It is said that in 1835, after a
raid by white hunters, the remaining inhabitants were
taken to the St. Gabrielle Mission, but not until 1855
was the solitary existence of Karana, the chief's daugh-
ter, discovered. She is buried in an unmarked grave
at Mission Santa Barbara.

Mission padres, only the sailors saw me rise
out of the grass, step onto the shore
in a dress of cormorant feathers, their green
sun-trembling, my black hair falling
royal to my hips. You sent them to

"rescue" me, the captured child who saved
herself: the plunge from the boat, the furtive
swim back. . . . You did not see the woman
who ran to the jetty, sprang
from rock to rock. You did not see her dive

into the ocean beyond the surf line, emerge
with abalone; you did not see her
smash the shell and tear the meat out
with her hands. I did not offer it to you. Monks,
as you led me away, only the sailors saw

my face, the desolate terrain, the bronzed look
I threw them over my shoulder, my eyes
as black as a nine-mile stretch of cold lava.
They would have taken me back.
Why did you accept me into mission life

if not to reunite me with my tribe
living so nearby. Because you
didn't know? Because I couldn't speak,
or wouldn't? High waves
and clouds of spray do not struggle.

Speak, you said. Didn't you hear me curse
your "God's will"? Didn't you hear
my wail, its echo fading into the fissures
of your mission: a sound
unlike anything you have ever heard?

I was never alone, blessed by walrus, heron,
sea lion, eagle, piper, pelican. . . . You think
you christened me. I christened myself
with sacred water brought on gale-storms,
by the spirits of my people

who were present on my island since
stone was soft. My hunted island,
barren now, grazed to the root by sheep, used
as a bombing target, pulverized
to sand. My island is not surprised when

one of its own wastes away. I was gone
in six weeks after stepping over
the gunwale of their boat. Wet grass
springs back, obliterates a footprint
as soon as the other foot is planted down.

My conversion vanished when you took
my feather dress and sent it to the Vatican.
When you caught me eating raw fish
stored in the cold-box,
and because I refused to wear

the ankle-length dress, walked nude
in your mission gardens, relieved myself
by your front door, you locked me away.
For the sake of decency, you said.
I had a language.

BY THE TRAIN STATION AT ASTRAPOVA

*Countess (Sonya) Tolstoy (1844-1919) was eleven
when she first met the family friend, Tolstoy. They
were married forty-eight years and had thirteen chil-
dren. When Sonya refused to adopt his changing be-
liefs, continued to pursue her business interests, and
social life, to attend concerts, he accused her of in-
fidelity and left. During the train ride to a monastery,
he caught pneumonia, and she traveled to be with him
before he died but was prevented. It became an inter-
national event, the first time newsreel cameras were
used.*

I pace beside the tracks, a word waiting
to be summoned, a scribble between the lines
on a page already written.

The roar of our years together
flashes by the newsreel. I need you as the film
needs the camera.

I beg the stationmaster to let me
wait in the small entryway of his hut,
only to crouch in a corner,

so the crowd will think I am visiting.
I have not come as wife,
but as peddler with pushcart,

or one of your pilgrims to pay homage,
to pray at your feet. I break from my keepers,
trample over my grief

spilling into the mud, stand on tiptoe
to catch a glimpse through the closed window.
Is it the kerosene lamp or you

who shed the light? Saint, prophet. . . .
I am as broken as a cup. I weep
for every splinter. Our thirteen

children: waltzes, polkas and quadrilles.
My favorite, gone like a little dance,
a quickstep kamaunskaya.

I have rewritten my life
in candlelight with each death, six
of our little ones, never loving

anyone but you. How could
your forehead reject my mouth,
your fingers disdain a touch.

I would sit by the fire
trance-lit. God, forgive me.
Everything.

&

THE WATCH BOOK

Elizabeth Parsons Ware Packard, 1863: arrested for religious heresy. Between 1840 and 1955, American law made it legal to confine women in hospitals without warning or trial.

I was beautiful when it was summer,
eight o'clock, when the doctor took
my pulse, when my neighbors saw
me banished from a clean tablecloth,
a window, the smell of mint. . . .

It is summer, eight o'clock; go to bed
ladies. The Watch Book has eyes,
a geography of mouth. What words
do the guards record in hours,
dateless years layered between

its hard covers, our foibles, their fancies?
Imaginations cut capers. That is all.
My children witnessed no caprice when
six men kidnapped me from my bed
in my nightgown: my husband's friend,

who enjoyed my singing, once; the judge
to whom our family paid a visit,
a little outing just last spring. . . . Walk,
ladies, walk. My clothes were taken,
the key, the door locked. No key

could fit my mouth. I disagreed, it's true.
When my mind renounced its churning,
the cream soured; when my thoughts rose,

the bread fell. No fancy the foible
in my husband's eyes yearning good-night

to her ankles as she stepped
from the carriage. I did not invent
four woman guards who held
another woman down, who beat her
because she could not dress herself.

Willfulness, the Watch Book records.
That invalid so stubborn,
they found her dead in the morning.
Walk, ladies. Walk.
My clothes are dead, but it wasn't me

who mangled them. I agree, I ripped
holes in all my sleeves,
patched them with notes: torn pleas,
scraps of travail concealed
by ribboned bands and bolts of lace

sewed with moonlight. Designs
no one ever read. Ten of us locked in
one room. Where are the other two?
Looking for their best clothes. How long
have they been missing? A day or two.

The Watch Book lies. They are not missing.
They died last year in the water closet.
That is all. Walk, ladies. I walk by
the window bars, those bars, the hands
of my clock. I am at the fourth grate

of summer, the third rectangle
at the corner of eight. I watch the sun rise,
the sun set. I kneel to Orion who walks
on the sea, pray to the Pleiades grieving
for their father who holds up the sky.

The sky, a book of watches.
Are those numbers free, set on their axes?
After three years, the guards set me free
to stroll alone in the yard. I look and look
into the face of summer as old as I,

as new as yesterday. A bird let out
in a room with the windows nailed shut,
I am my feet, my feet are wings. With a new
geography of ear, eye, mouth, I am headless,
cutting capers. It is eight o'clock. Time for bed.

That is all, is all.

SUFFRAGE, 1917: IMPRISONED FOR OBSTRUCTING TRAFFIC

*When suffragettes were arrested they usually refused
as a matter of policy to pay the fine and go free. All
the same, some of the women lacked legal representa-
tion, others were without family, friends, or financial
resources. Once jailed, many were refused commu-
nication with the outside world.*

1

I could not sleep thinking of the girl
partly suspended and strapped

to the greasy pole, her hands bound
behind her, hour after hour

slipping slowly down. Officer,
were her arms finally pulled

from their sockets? The doctor
is trying to pull my mind

from its socket. I have never been
afraid of anything: our warrantless

arrest for obstructing traffic while we stood
on Pennsylvania Avenue, deserted

after the procession; my nakedness
when they refuse to let me

wear my nightgown; I fear neither
the spoonfuls of worms I scoop

from the surface of my soup every day
nor the finale of our hunger strike:

a tube pushed down my throat, food
dropping like lead to my stomach, vomit

spilling down my neck; I do not
even fear the small light the doctor

holds to my face. But I am afraid
of the light in the doctor's eyes.

2

Life in this solitary cell is
my blanket unwashed for a year.
How we all long for fresh air.

Officer, would you draw on
your rubber gloves and change
my bedsheet? For this, I would give

my treasured book of Browning,
but a week ago, in our fight for air,
we threw all we had at the window,

twenty feet away
from eighty of us crowded,
tier upon tier, in one room: shoes,

tin drinking cups, a mirror. . . .
The bouquet in that October gust
almost knocked us over.

I was more grateful to the poet
for the weight of the paper in his book
than for the weight in his words.

Can you blame our little group
dedicated to rebellion when
our sons are sent to fight for freedom

in Europe? My own, the nerve
of my heart, his abundance
could, even now, be wasting into

a foreign soil. Although he is
farther away than my mind
can fathom, I am not going mad.

3

The stench you smell is from the pail. My toilet
has not yet been emptied. Thank you for
the bedsheet. Thank you for a blanket,
washed. Thank you for the water in this leaky

cup, my third and last today. I will
follow the trail like a scent, lapping up
each drop you spilled along the hall when I
go back for the investigation of my sanity.

The doctor will capture trophies from my mind
like the golden shreds of our freedom-banners
small boys save. How is your world
beyond these bars? Do you have news

of more disorder in the capital, do you have
a sister? Each hour, day
and night, nurses observe me,
convinced I have persecution mania.

The door-sound clanks on my bones,
the light snaps sharp on my face. Others
shuffle by on their way to the insane asylum
without trial, counsel, or kindness.

4

Once I spoke with Maria Moravsky,
the touring poet from czarist Russia.
She was twice in solitary, but respected,
not beaten, allowed to wear her own clothes,
to wash, to read and write. Officer,

I would love a piece of paper even more
than a clean bedsheet. A pen perhaps.
No ink. I could use the blood we wiped up
off the floor of the booby house and scrubbed
from our sister's clothes after her beating.

I can't imagine what harm she caused fighting
back on nothing but water for nineteen days—
Oh, the ladies are building a song again
to the tune of an old sea-shanty. Listen,
cell by cell, line by line, *the voiceless and the free*. . . .

‰

AFTER TWENTY-ONE YEARS

*Vera Figner, born in 1852 to Russian nobility, be-
came a member of the Executive Committee for The
Will of the People party. In 1883 she was arrested for
plotting the assassination of Alexander II and sen-
tenced to life. Because of her mother's youthful ac-
quaintance with the emperor, Vera was released from
the Schlusselburg Fortress, 1904.*

Home is a fortress where your name,
brought to its knees by a number,
is forgotten, where inmates one by one
hang themselves or go mad,
where rosy-cheeked sister, and beardless brother
turn to cobwebs you hold on to spanning
twenty-one years, their deaths bringing
only regret. Home is a customary place, known,

a comprehension in its dumb stone,
where walls speak to everyone
but the insane, when each year's passing
is recorded at Christmas, and years pass
without paper to record it, where all
you have left is your mother's words,
and the locket she pressed
in the palm of your hand, inscribed

on its porcelain: *most holy Virgin of joy
unexpected.* Home is the wasted
and melancholy earth, put to death, hardening
in its sterility, where you plead with
forgotten eloquence to create,

behind the fences, a garden, and a friend
draws designs for it from blue plaster
scraped from the walls, and soot. Home is where

you learn your mother's deathbed appeal
to the emperor's mercy has finally
been granted, but you wait for your release
while tree sprigs break through
chips and bark and greenery sprouts
from the rocks, until your mother is lowered
into the earth. At last, when you are released,
when the door scrapes behind you, when you see

bushes swelling from burdock, flowers springing
from nettle, there holding to clods of limestone,
thriving in gravel, the garden as fragile as
the words carved on the case, as her hair
in the locket, as healing as her voice after the trial—
may even you have the joy of the unexpected—
tears you thought you had laid to rest rise
from their graves protesting. You look up

at the window. Like the gendarme
compelled by duty to witness an execution,
you stop at the threshold, clutch at the gate.
Your honor, spare me, I cannot go on,
I cannot bear it. Above the scaffold,
your comrades' pale faces press against
that pane, mouthing to one of their daughters.
Hands flutter, shrink a powdery farewell.

❧

KIM'S STORY

North Korean terrorist Kim Hyon Hui placed a bomb on a South Korean Airliner. She was captured and sentenced to death in 1989 by the Seoul government, which later granted her a special pardon for propaganda purposes. She lives in protective custody, always in danger of being assassinated.

One hundred and sixteen blew up
above the Andaman Sea. The bomb
was in the overnight bag I left aboard—
while their bodies were being contorted
by the force of the explosive plummet,
I was trying on new clothes
in the airport's duty-free shop, turning
this way and that to get a matching
size in the mirror: I thought,
I was free; I thought,

They'll never catch me now, I'll never
have to use the cyanide capsule
in the filter of my cigarette,
supplied by my superiors:
that Marlboro memento is still in a pocket,
tucked away with my northern life.

Now I gaze north toward Kwanmo
Mountain, certain it keeps my mother's tears
in its rivers, those rivers that flow south
into the Yellow Sea. I am
the "Land of the Morning Calm, Korea,"
my borders divided by generations
of crime, centuries of war . . . .

My southern captors trot me out
for propaganda occasions, to lecture
the rebellious students, to tell my story over
and over: How they selected me
in childhood, how I was trained

to obey their evil designs, trained
as a terrorist. Each morning I had to dust
my compound's painting of Him,
our dictator, our North Korean god.
(I'm trying to forget his name.) How
honored I was to receive His holy mission.
I embraced my special task, the atrocity
bestowed on me like a fortunate
marriage, the bomb whose works I
never did understand, but that was all right;
all I had to do, stow it up there
in the overhead compartment.
My audiences tend to wince at this point.

Repentance rewards: given a new life,
pardoned into protective custody,
kept secure with monthly paychecks
from the Information Ministry, I live
in a "safe house," a refuge to which
each day they forward my mail:
marriage proposals, death threats,
invitations to tea. Men want me.
I am a Virgin Terrorist.
They dream of me, their eyes flower
like flak, like festival fireworks. But
I am not a fascination, I am a machine.

They push my buttons, North
and South, both there and here they
turn me this way and that to suit
their doctrines, educating, reeducating,
constructing, patiently correcting my faults.

Former comrade, dutiful party daughter,
now I sit in the interviewee's
chair, the Seoul TV studio bright and hot
around me, the lights detonating
my eyes. The makeup girl fusses
above me, adjusting the new gold crucifix
at my throat, clipping my hair back
with a pearl, touching up my mouth,
inventing my perfections.

❧

FOUR: THE INNOCENT/THE GUILTY

THE ARSENIC EATER

The Scene: 1840, following the second trial of Hannah Kinney, who allegedly poisoned her two husbands. Both died of arsenic poisoning; however, as arsenic was often prescribed for syphilis, it was unclear whether she had poisoned her husbands or not and was acquitted.

I was the needlewoman bound to him,
the coveted prize.
The lawyers said I had no reason,
no motive to hate my husband: drunkard,
gambler, victim of disease,

torpid in his opium.
Ruined fortune. Body as broken
as the ties of our marriage: bled,
leeched, blistered. I applied
mustard poultices to his feet, abdomen.

The one mind said, I must be
his tonic, his Swaim's Panacea,
welcome him into my heart.
For him I had to be the hilltop
of first light on first snow,

as white as the sediment left by arsenic.
When he deserted me that time,
oh yes, I did exchange
the hired boy for a hired man.
Ah, the hey-day.

Although in court they said I was just
"an ordinary crust of bread," it's true:
some called me beautiful. My sex,
my respectable rank.
I doled out pills

made of mustard and cayenne pepper,
that was all.
Only a little herb tea.
Both Boston water and Boston sugar
leave a white sediment, they said,

and cleared my name.
The courtroom crowd rose up
and cheered to the "law's chivalry."
We all played out the drama.
But the one mind knew,

the mind of kitchens
and bedrooms
that gives the game away—
the white granules
in his stomach could not argue.

❧

MY HEART BEATS IN WILD RAPTURE FOR YOU: COME PREPARED TO STAY FOREVER

> *Belle Gunness (1860-1908?), serial killer, found her victims through lonely hearts ads that promised marriage. After Belle's house burned down, and her children's bodies and a woman's body were discovered in the ruins, her handyman and lover was charged with the crime. Belle was never heard of again, though there were many subsequent "sightings."*

Like explorers following a trade route
my lovers came. No vile despoilers
answered my honey-kissed ad.
They dug out their lives' savings

from the local banks as boggle-eyed
as the deputies who unearthed
the bones and eleven men's watches
in my hog pen. A plague-pit

of scab-crust and quicklime. Like triflers
who need not apply, the winds rose
over those soft spots under
my lilacs: books on anatomy, hypnotism.

Ashes stole off on the lam by the burned
butcher shop where I slaughtered
the hogs in my overalls. More bodies
cut up, wrapped in gunnysacks

fell away under their shovels: forty-two
lying out in the red carriage shed.
When deputies found my teeth
in the smolder, the whole village mourned,

poor widow and her charred children.
They accused my handyman,
the lover I fired, the one who bragged
in the bar, the same night

I burned down my house, ripped out
the stump of my real anchor tooth
with the false plate still
attached and threw it all into the blaze.

Now I live the high life in New York
disguised as a man while he rots
spitting blood in a cell. He always said,
What china blue eyes you have.

THE SNOW-WHITE DOVE: "HAPLESS, HELPLESS, AND FORLORN"

North Carolina, 1850. Although acquitted for the poisoning death of her husband, Ann Simpson was almost certainly guilty of that murder.

I prepared a tasty coffee for you,
darling; you always said you liked it
strong and sweet. Not like our boarder.
That's why I told him to pass the cup
along to you. I did not say it sharply,
did I? I clearly saw you would sicken
and die when I read your tea leaves.
Our old town witch said the same.
He will die within a week, she said,
then you will have the man
you have always loved.

Darling, you closed your eyes
for three years, three years
before you "discovered" us,
and then you hit me. It made our marriage
unreliable like the chemical tests,
contaminated. I was the dirty vessel.
Emotions, like the experts, are not
completely trustworthy, you know.
I flew to the jury's bosom.
They weren't so dastardly to hang a woman.
They cherished me, protected me.

Wasn't I a lady?
Were they such fools
to find me, a mere girl, a weeping widow

collapsed in her mother's arms, guilty:
I was hapless, helpless, friendless,
and forlorn, they said. Yes, I had been
skittish perhaps, a little selfish, somewhat
indiscreet; your jealousy unfounded.
These things happen,
as my attorney said, in other lands,
darling, not in North Carolina.

❧

WHEN I WAS AN EGGSHELL

Pamela and Paul Sainsbury lived for eight years in the outskirts of Sidmouth, South Devon, England. She confided the murder to her neighbor, who went to the police. Although Pamela confessed, the DNA testing was inconclusive, as the remains of Paul's body had been buried for eight months. On December 13,1991, she was sentenced to two years' probation.

The garden earth too hard to dig,
I left him in the cornfield
behind the hedge. I used to watch you
go out walking in it
all by yourself, dreamed of going. . . .

One autumn I tried. When I saw
the corn borers had destroyed it, I feared
they might latch on to me
and came straight home. You say
I look Victorian

in my old-fashioned clothes,
my hair pulled back. You didn't see
the nude photos he made me pose for
or hear him snarl, I'll show these
to the world, your family.

I'll burn down their house if you
even think of leaving. Wrapped up
his head with those photos, dropped it
in a plastic bag, kept it on the shelf
with the hats for eight months

to remind me . . . the scars on my hands
from pulling the cord will never let me
forget, and neighbors like you could never
guess by them what went on. I would have
said hello to you more often,

but he didn't like me having friends,
especially married-woman ones like you.
You draw asterisks on your calendar
for special times. I've drawn
two on mine, one for the trip I made

from house to field with him
chopped up in the wheelbarrow, and one
for the drunken night he threw me
downstairs and jumped on my leg—
the night I crossed my Rubicon.

I tied a nylon cord loose in his tool-bag,
a plumb line to the bedpost, coiled it
round his neck and pulled.
I garroted his rage. After I used
his tenon-saw with the foot-long blade,

you would not have thought
my floors so spotless, curtains
so fresh, walls so white.
Worked on the bedroom floor
four days just as I worked

when he made me saw the wood
for the front gate, when I lost
my will to run away,
when I was an eggshell.
I wanted to say—

You eat, you sleep, you talk, you
lead a nice life. Look at the life
I'm leading—but I never spoke a word
he didn't understand
or he'd beat me. I grunted

as I trussed his remains in those
three black garbage-bags, just as I grunted
when he made me strip naked,
buckled a dog collar round my neck,
and watched me eat from a bowl on the floor.

ॐ

THE ALMIGHTY FIREBALL

Kiranjit Ahluwalia received a life sentence for murder, but after three years in prison and months of counseling by The Pragna Patel, a women's group, she revealed the details of her marriage. Her cultural and religious background prevented the family from giving evidence at the trial. On September 25, 1992, after a second trial at the Old Bailey, London, England, Ahluwalia was released.

I won't go shopping. I won't visit friends.
I won't dye my hair. I won't eat hot chili.
I won't ask for help, if you don't like it.
I won't try to kill myself. I won't drink
Black coffee, talk to neighbors. I won't
Laugh if you don't want me to. I won't return
To law school, study, read my books. Please
Don't break the milk jug. I won't try
To run away when you say, Come on, run
Here, you bastard. You don't have to push it
In my stomach. I won't sweep the pieces
When you throw the cups and plates.
I won't try to kill myself—
When you pulled me by the hair

Into the car's backseat to poke out my eyes
With the screwdriver, I escaped
To your mother and she said, Don't tell,
Don't tell: the boiling tea, broken teeth, fingers,
Handfuls of hair ripped out, welts
From buckle-ends of belts. Your brothers
Chose him for you. Don't dishonor
The families. But their invocation of the Izzat

Does not make you Hanuman.
You are not a mountain made a god. You
Did not lead Rama to rescue his
Beautiful bride lost to a demon. You
Held my face down on the ironing board,
Pressed the red-hot iron to my cheek.

Either you will die or I will. I will
Save money for my funeral, wear
Western clothes, pray to God and my father—
I will do a prison-pilgrimage to wash my sins.
Give you a fire-bath to wash your own.
I will fill the diaper pail with oil, pour it on
The quilt under which you sleep. I will wear
An oven glove. From the gas cooker, I will light
A candle, throw it on your feet.
Instead of running after me, your feet
Will run in pursuit of your shrieks. Like
The raised scar on my face, your ashes
Will scar the road, and the wind
Will scatter them without care, perfumes, or rites.

ॐ

MA BARKER AND HER GANG:
HERMAN, ARTHUR, FREDDY,
KARPIS (CREEPY) & LOYD (DOC)

*Ma Barker (1872–1935) and her sons were some of
the most vicious and elusive killers who roamed
throughout the midwest during the 1930s. Among
their crimes: murdering with abandon, robbing banks,
and kidnapping millionaires.*

All right, boys, go ahead, I yelled. No teargas bombs will
rout us out. We'll die at our posts. Let the damn Feds
have it. Shoot—

It took you fourteen bullets to kill my Freddy,
buried in a bed of shells, fourteen,
and three for me. But the plug in my heart,

I put there myself. One for my darling Herman trailed
by you but never snared. Injured,
he blasted his brains out in his car in a ditch in Wichita.

After that, you said I got real mean. Harridan,
you called me, Beast. Didn't I round up my livestock,
herd them off to Sunday school every single week

until those snooty churchgoers blabbered on about
vandals? Their precious private property. Sure, I said,
my boys will fight, they'll steal, they'll do a little damage,

but they're good boys and mind me. You mind your own
business. I quit church. We moved to Webb City.
All's I wanted, just a place they'd stand a better chance

of growing up without being persecuted. You lawmen
never stopped picking on my spawn. Didn't I
get them cleared every time you louts came

pounding on our door? Don't you dare call my boys
highway robbers, they're just a little wild, active,
that's all. If you farts

don't cut my offspring loose, I'll go to the governor
of the state, get every single one of you kicked
off the force. I tell you, my boys was marked—

So, I made sure my brood was reared by the bravest
swindlers and border bandits of our time.
A trail of gun slingers drifted in and out of our settlings,

social as termites: gambling, drinking, educating my boys.
Crime was their work, the law their enemy.
Their heritage: a long line of quick getaways.

We just kept moving. Like the seasons, we weren't trees.
On one of those treks, you hypocrites
robbed us of everything: my Bible, chamber pot,

my old dolls in the trunk. You even stole the kids'
yellowing report cards: their failing grades. All counterfeits.
My fry was smarter than the whole lot of you, Feds, lawmen,

And they was loyal, too. When my Freddy and his lover
Karpis—we called him Creepy after his facial alteration—
when they weren't knocking over banks they were

scouting out young gals to bring home
for me to knock around. Devoted to their Ma, they were.
When I finished having sex I'd say, Get rid of her, boys.

They'd just up and kill her. The bodies of those young girls
still float across the cold Minnesota lakes.
Freddy'd pop the eyes out of any copper he saw

coming toward his car 'cause he thought
his lover might be knocked off too. My Freddy dropped
a lot of people to save his sweetheart. All my boys

was kill-crazy lovers. You called them crackpots,
reported I was nothing but a mumbling, fat old lady
who couldn't lay out breakfast—you listen.

I went off to listen to Amos and Andy when they went off
to plot and plan 'cause it was me who cased the banks.
You got to know people to get along.

I knew about people. Could bring around officials anywhere.
Those folks bent over backwards when I said, I am
a law-abiding oil woman with a large deposit;

how does your system hook up? Some brainless poke
would always show this hoaxter the alarms,
wires, where the armed guards stood. . . . But, when

you Feds plastered up those *Wanted* posters everywhere,
you made my youngsters stars. Why, my boys got
so famous they had to change their faces.

Old sawbones sliced away the fat, tucked folds of skin
behind their ears, pulled it over bone tighter
than rawhide over a drum. He scraped their fingers

with his scalpel sharper than the ends of pencils.
He was so sloshed when he did the job,
their botched faces, their grotesque scars made them

twice as ugly as when he started. Besides, the mooch
gossiped to a prostitute, bragged he'd haul a fortune
for turning us in. My clan took the old bore

out for a ride, gave him a taste of his own medicine;
dumped him in a hole and covered it with lime.
Anyone who talks to whores is too dangerous to live.

I saw you crouched behind your cars, the trees.
Fourteen agents and the state police. You saw me
at the upstairs window. We was ready for battle.

I stuffed Loyd's I'll-see-you-soon postcard
into my handbag. Set it stuffed with ten thousand
legal tender by the window. Propped my gas-generated

automatic, a ninety-four rounder, on the sill and hollered,
All right boys, go ahead. No teargas bombs will rout us out.
We'll die at our posts. Let the damn Feds have it. Shoot—

ళ

ACKNOWLEDGMENTS

A tribute to my children Evangelene and Cullen for accepting their disruptive other sibling, my computer, for their evenings of cooking and the games I didn't go to, for their patient listening, their questions, wonder, and for being there right from the beginning. Praise to my sister Cullene Bryant, for her wisdom, strength and the sound of her voice every week over the wires crossing the continent.

Special thanks to the BOA team responsible for this book's publication, Steve Huff for his assurance, Thom Ward for his enthusiasm and sensitivity; I am grateful.

With fond appreciation to friends and teachers, past and present: Nancy Christie of Toronto and childhood who read my first poems, Richard Noonan for his phone-call contributions, Joan Houlihan for our Saturday-night-writing exercises, and Ed Owens for those computers and printers. Thanks to Irene Harris, Margarite Rumas, Colin Bourn at Fitchburg State College for their feedback on this manuscript, and to Jerry Green in the library for guiding my first curiosity at the front Research desk, by way of lists, books, and newspapers, to the dark side and obsession. A heartfelt thanks to Lucie Brock-Broido and my buddies in our oldies workshop (newies, too) who were the first to read many of these poems. With affectionate memories for all those at Emerson College in Boston, there and gone. I am fortunate to have studied with Marie Howe, Mary Carr, and Tom Lux. Above all, my deep appreciation to Bill Knott for his devotion to my quest, his humorous encouragement and zeal for these poems, for his editing assistance, suggestions, and the title. Love and many thanks. Also, I can't forget the Edna St. Vincent Millay Colony. These poems are for all of you.

Finally, I am indebted to the following books and their authors: *From Cradle to Grave* by Joyce Egginton; *Memoirs of a Revolutionist* by Vera Figner; *Murder for Love* by Ione Quinby; *Sex Espionage* by David E. Bower; *Sonya: The Life of Countess Tolstoy* by Ann Edwards; *The Final Struggle; Being Countess Tolstoy's Diary for 1910*, Sergey Lvovich Tolstoy, editor; *The Witchcraft Delusion in Colonial Connecticut, 1647–*

1697 by John M. Taylor, edited by Maurice Filler; *When Women Kill* by Coramae Richey Mann, edited by David Luckenbill; *Women and Madness* by Phyllis Chesler. I am beholden particularly to Ann Jones for her invaluable *Women Who Kill*, which first opened my eyes, inspired and spawned these poems.

My sincere thanks to the editors of the following publications in which some of these poems first appeared:

Explorations: "My Father Sold Me to Pay His Debts" (published as "The Indentured Servant");
Larcome Review: "The Watch Book";
Madison Review: "God Is a Cowboy Who Rides a Lame Horse," "Suffrage, 1917: Imprisoned for Stopping Traffic";
Mississippi Review: "Nine Stones."

❧

ABOUT THE AUTHOR

Suzanne Owens grew up in Toronto, Canada. She graduated from the University of Western Ontario and received her MFA in writing from Emerson College, Boston. A graduate of the American Musical and Dramatic Academy, New York, Owens has been a member of Actor's Equity, the Screen Actors Guild, and worked as an actress in England, Canada, and the United States. She has developed a one-woman play based on the characters in this book. Owens won the Frank Cat Press Chapbook Award, 1996, for *Theater Poems*, and resides in Massachusetts, teaching poetry, writing and acting in the Boston area.

෨෴

BOA EDITIONS, LTD.

THE A. POULIN, JR. NEW POETS OF AMERICA SERIES

COLOPHON

The Daughters of Discordia, poems by Suzanne Owens,
with a foreword by Denise Duhamel,
was set using Goudy fonts and Monotype Arabesque Ornaments
by Richard Foerster, York Beach, Maine.
The cover was designed by Rishma Goa.
Manufacturing was by McNaughton & Gunn,
Saline, Michigan.

Special support for this book came from the following
individuals and organizations:
Debra Audet, Brad & Debra Dean,
Richard Garth & Mimi Hwang, Dane & Judy Gordon,
Robert & Willie Hursh, Meg Kearney,
Archie & Pat Kutz, Francie & Robert Marx,
Boo Poulin, Alva & Irene Royston,
Pat & Michael Wilder, Sabra Wood.

❧